Land of Legend

CLIVE WADDINGTON

Land of Legend

Copyright © 1997 the Country Store.
All rights reserved. This book is protected by copyright. No part of it may be reproduced, stored in a retrieval system, or transmitted in any form or by any means, electronic, mechanical photocopying or otherwise, without the written permission of the Publisher.

ISBN 0 9530163 0 7

Published by:- The Country Store, Main Road, Milfield, Wooler, Northumberland, NE71 6JD
Telephone : 01668 216535

Front Cover: Duddo Fourstones Stone Circle

Land of Legend. Discovering the heart of Ancient Northumberland

Introduction

The heartland of ancient Northumberland is centred on the Till Valley, a fertile plain overlooked by the mighty Cheviot Hills to the west and an enclosing sandstone ridge to the east. Known locally as Glendale, or the Milfield basin, this landscape contains a wealth of extraordinary archaeological remains. This unique story of past human settlement has left its imprint on the landscape in the form of upstanding monuments, ancient carvings, and the remains of flint tools and ancient pottery which can still be found in the soil.

Aerial photographs have revealed an extremely rich buried archaeological landscape in the Basin, making its significance comparable to the better known remains of Wessex. The area known as the Milfield Basin, the catchment of the rivers Till and Glen (see map), has outstanding archaeological remains dating, in particular, to the Neolithic, Bronze Age, Iron Age and early Medieval periods.

However, this story of past human settlement is not just detectable from archaeological residues. For example, the study of ancient pollen furnishes archaeologists with information about how the landscape was exploited, whether pastoral, arable or forestry, as well as what type of crops were grown.

It is the job of the archaeologist to piece together all these fragments of information, whether from archaeological remains, environmental evidence or written historical accounts, and construct an understanding of the past. It is intended that through an enhanced understanding of the archaeology of the area, both in terms of its historic importance and its vulnerability to modern developments, sensitive management of this valuable landscape will be achieved.

Equally, it is hoped that the great historic importance of this area will be reinstated and its unique and exciting history made more widely known.

Chronology

History did not start with the Romans! Far from it, people have lived and exploited the British Isles, including the Milfield Basin, for thousands of years previously, as highly developed societies.

It is only since the retreat of the last ice sheets, about 10,000 years ago, that cultural remains are encountered in the north from which past life can be recreated and interpreted. The period from the end of the last glaciation up to about 4000BC is known as the **Mesolithic** (the middle stone-age) and is usually characterised as a period during which hunting, gathering and fishing communities moved around the landscape in association with the seasons, often with more permanent settlement along coastal areas by the latter part of the period.

From about 4000BC up to about 2000BC the **Neolithic** (new stone-age) period is characterised by a significant ideological shift which included the construction of impressive burial mounds and later, massive stone, timber and earthen religious monuments, as well as the first use of domesticated animals and plants - that is, the introduction of farming.

Although the first use of metal, usually for prestige objects, took place during the late Neolithic, the **Bronze Age**, from 2000BC to about 700BC, also witnessed the establishment of permanent stone and timber settlements and farms with field boundaries and paddocks. Bronze was used to make tools, weapons and display objects, though many other metals including gold and silver were also used, the exception being iron. The emergence of a more strictly stratified society took place with an emerging division between secular and sacred activities an important development from the all pervading ritual and ceremony of the Neolithic.

The **Iron Age**, which brackets the period from about 700BC until about 80AD saw the reinforcement of the trends emerging by the late Bronze Age, with enlarged tribal groupings and ultimately the development of highly organized kingdoms for which we have names, thanks to Roman writers. The land was intensively farmed and the use of iron plough shares made an important contribution to agricultural practice. Iron also provided a stronger and more widely available material for forging the weaponry of the warrior class and the tools of the artisans. It was during this period that many of the local hillforts such as Yeavering Bell and Dod Law were constructed.

The period from 80 AD until 410AD is referred to as the **Romano-British** period - covering the Roman occupation of the north, even though for most of this period the Milfield Basin and North Northumberland lay beyond the Roman empire. Although this is probably the least well understood period in this area, settlement and subsistence strategies appear to have continued in a similar fashion to the preceding Iron Age, though contact with the Roman empire must have had a significant effect, even if only on the psychology of residents who now found themselves living in a frontier zone.

The **Early Medieval** period, sometimes and inaccurately referred to as the Dark Ages, extends from 410 AD until 1066 and the arrival of the Normans. This period witnessed continuous power struggles between competing dynasties of Britons and Angles and external powers such as the Mercians of the Midlands, the Picts, Scots, Welsh, and later the Vikings. However, it also saw a great flowering of Anglo-British culture and learning, manifest in the writing of the monk Bede and the scriptoria at Lindisfarne, Monkwearmouth and Jarrow. In addition, the period saw the spread of Northumbrian Christianity to what is now Germany by the endeavours of Willibrord and St.Boniface.

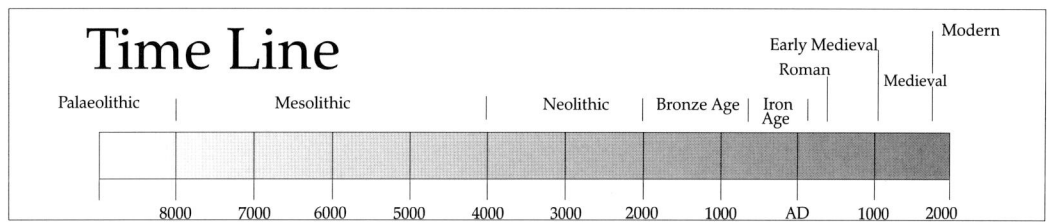

It is important, however, to bear in mind that these historical periods, particularly the pre- Roman ones, are just a convenient way by which archaeologists break up the past on the basis of technology (bronze, iron and so on) rather than by subsistence, or social changes, for example. Of course, people who lived at the time did not consider themselves as 'Mesolithic', or 'Neolithic' and it is likely their notion of time itself was different from ours; where we envisage time as a linear process (the 'arrow of time'), they are more likely to have envisaged time as a cycle similar to the annual cycles of the natural world.

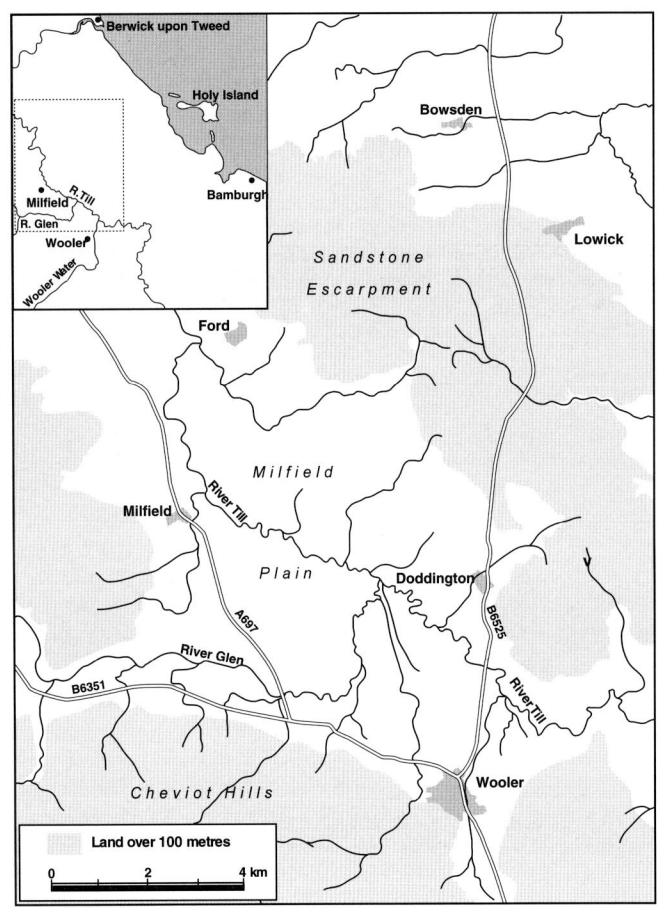

Location Map

The heartland of ancient Northumberland is centred upon the Till Valley in north Northumberland - known locally as part of Glendale.

Based upon the Ordnance Survey mapping with the permission of The Controller of Her Majesty's Stationery Office   © Crown copyright (85-49)

The Mesolithic

As the ice sheets retreated and the glacial conditions gave way to a warmer climate, large quantities of gravels were washed down with the meltwaters from the hills of the Cheviot massif.

These gravels were deposited on the valley floor forming a fan which spread out from the mouth of Glendale in a similar fashion to a river delta. It is these relatively flat raised gravel terraces which have been particularly attractive for settlement from the early post-glacial period up to and including the present day. The village of Milfield is itself located on this gravel surface.

The glacial meltwaters formed a vast lake (Lake Ewart) on the valley floor beyond the gravel deposits, extending over what is now the modern flood plain of the rivers Till and Glen; an area of about 16-20 square km ! Soon after 8000BC the lake eventually drained away when the water body broke through the sandstone escarpment at Etal, thus creating the gorge there and allowing the Lake and the river Till to drain into the Tweed to the north.

The lowest parts of the valley floor, on the margins of the rivers Glen and Till, developed into carr (marshy wetlands) offering rich resources to human communities, such as wildfowl and fish. Quantities of Mesolithic stone tools have been recovered from the gravel surfaces adjacent to what was then the carr land, indicating that mobile groups of hunter-gatherer-fishermen made camp in clearings on the well draining gravel surface, probably during

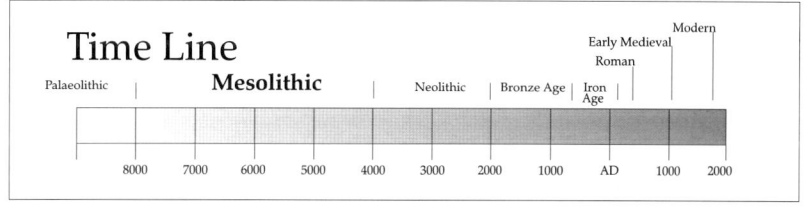

the summer months, to exploit these resources. Their homes are thought to have consisted of tent structures made from animal hides with a wooden frame with an internal hearth and working areas outside. While certain members of these family groups made home on the valley floor, more specialist task groups roamed the wooded uplands where wild animals such as auroch (wild cattle), red deer, roe deer and wild pig could be hunted for their meat, hides, sinew and bone - all of which could be utilised for making tents, clothes and tools as well as providing a good quality food, high in protein. In addition, nuts, berries, fruits of the forest and some grasses were collected to supplement the diet.

These roaming hunting groups were highly mobile and would spend the night at places which could offer a degree of natural shelter. In the case of the Milfield Basin the outcropping cliffs of the sandstone escarpment to the east of the river Till were used by such groups as rock shelter sites where transitory encampments, in the form of lean-to structures, were erected against the rock face. Excavations at the base of Goatscrag, Corbys Crag and at Bowden Doors have revealed remains of these occupations.

There is very little naturally occurring flint in Northumberland, except for the small pebbles of beach flint which can be collected from the coast where they are washed in from their source area in Scandinavia. This accounts for why many of the tools so far recovered, which date to this period, are made from the locally available, though poorer quality, cherts, agates, quartz and volcanic material (which can be collected from the gravel deposits in the Milfield Plain). The flint tools tend to be small and of beach flint, implying that this flint was brought inland from the coast, probably when family groups moved towards the coast during the winter months, where the ameliorating effects of the sea make the coast attractive for settlement by reducing the winter extremes experienced inland. Some food such as meat and fish was preserved for the winter months by smoking and drying. Boats made of skins and fish weirs and bone harpoons were used to catch fish in coastal areas.

The use of local resources indicates relatively small cohesive self-reliant social groups, probably of extended families, living in this area. These smaller units probably aggregated into larger units, or bands, at certain times of the year to settle differences, seek marriage partners, exchange commodities, observe rituals and reinforce allegiances. Studies of modern-day hunter-gatherer communities elsewhere in the world (ethnography) indicate that such groups possess a very detailed understanding of the landscape/s they inhabit and that their beliefs about the world and their place within it were mapped on to the landscape by imbuing natural features of the landscape with the names and myths which constituted those beliefs about the world. Thus, natural features such as rivers, waterfalls, prominent hills and mountains, exposed sheets of bedrock would, by being invested with such meaning, act as constant reminders of their beliefs and their sense of being in the world. Through this symbolic ordering of the landscape, cultural memory was preserved and passed down through generations by the learning of myths and beliefs associated with each part of the landscape within their annual round. In such societies land is rarely owned, though territorial rights to certain areas often serve to divide up the landscape on a symbolic basis and at a very broad scale, between say, the hunting grounds of one band and those of another.

Although more susceptible to the variations in climate, and lacking the security and luxuries with which we are familiar, this free and nomadic existence offered qualities of life of a completely different nature from those with which we are accustomed to today.

What is an Auroch ?

Aurochsen were the wild cattle in Britain before the rearing of domesticated stock. These fearsome animals were approximately 1.5 times as large as modern cattle and weighed around 1,400 kg. They usually roamed the landscape singly and were grazing and browsing animals.

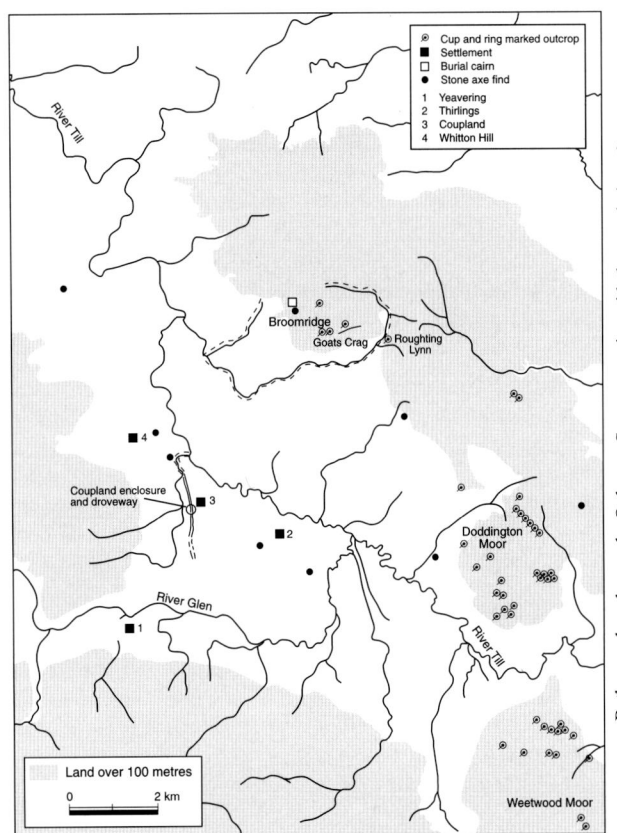

Early Neolithic Sites in the Milfield Basin

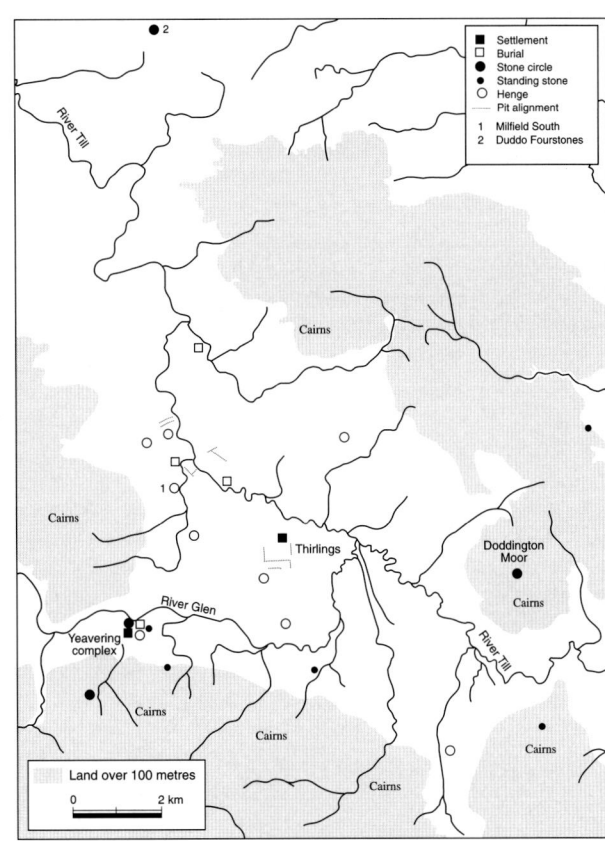

Late Neolithic Sites in the Milfield Basin

The Neolithic

By the later fifth millennium BC, a number of changes took place which altered the way people thought about the world, the structure of social relations, together with innovations in the procurement of foodstuffs and the way the landscape was exploited. However, it is necessary to stress that there was also much continuity with the preceding period.

Although the climatic optimum had been reached during the Mesolithic c.6500BC, when the average winter and summer temperatures were around two degrees centigrade higher than today, the deterioration in climate between then and about 2000BC was only gradual and spasmodic.

People started rearing domesticated livestock and cultivating domesticated plant foods for the first time from around 4000BC onwards. This took place in addition to continued hunting, fishing and the seasonal exploitation of different parts of the landscape.

Cattle and pig are browsing animals and are, in fact, natural creatures of the forest. Small clearings provide additional grazing where such animals tend to aggregate. These areas on the wooded sandstone uplands were used as the summer grazing areas for the domestic herds of the early Neolithic pastoral-hunting communities which inhabited the Milfield Basin.

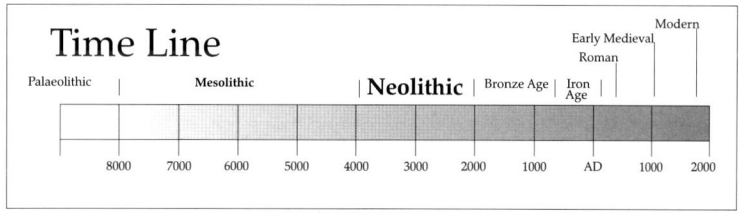

Cup and Ring Marks

The prehistoric rock art known as 'cup and ring marks' were carved on the exposed bedrock located in these clearings on the sandstone fells. They probably expressed ideological beliefs associated with the successful maintenance of the pastoral cycle and in so doing the clearings were marked out as important ritual places no doubt related to the upkeep of the regenerative powers of nature. The livestock were driven off the fells and down to the main settlement areas on the valley floor for over-wintering, calving and slaughter at certain times of the year.

Earliest henge type monument in Britain

Recent excavations to the south of Milfield village on the Coupland Enclosure (a massive circular earthwork with two entrances), have produced evidence of a large droveway and stock enclosure dating to this period. This important monument, its remains now buried, extends over a hectare in area and was the place where the herds from the uplands were driven at certain times of the year. It is probable that this pastoral system, and the Coupland monument in particular, were included in a ritual scheme associated with this subsistence system (see illustration on opposite page). The early dates for the construction of this monument makes it the **earliest henge-like enclosure in Britain, predating Stonehenge by hundreds of years** and, as such, although functioning in the pastoral regime, probably provides the structural form from which the henge tradition developed. Consequently this monument, the largest early Neolithic enclosure so far known in the north, is therefore one of the most significant Neolithic sites in Britain!

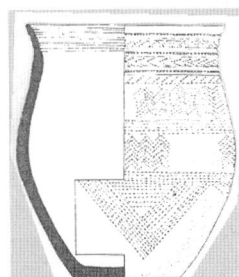

Late Neolithic Beaker (found Chatton Moor)

Small cultivation plots in clearings on the well-draining tractable soils which fringe the Milfield Plain, particularly on the western side of the valley around

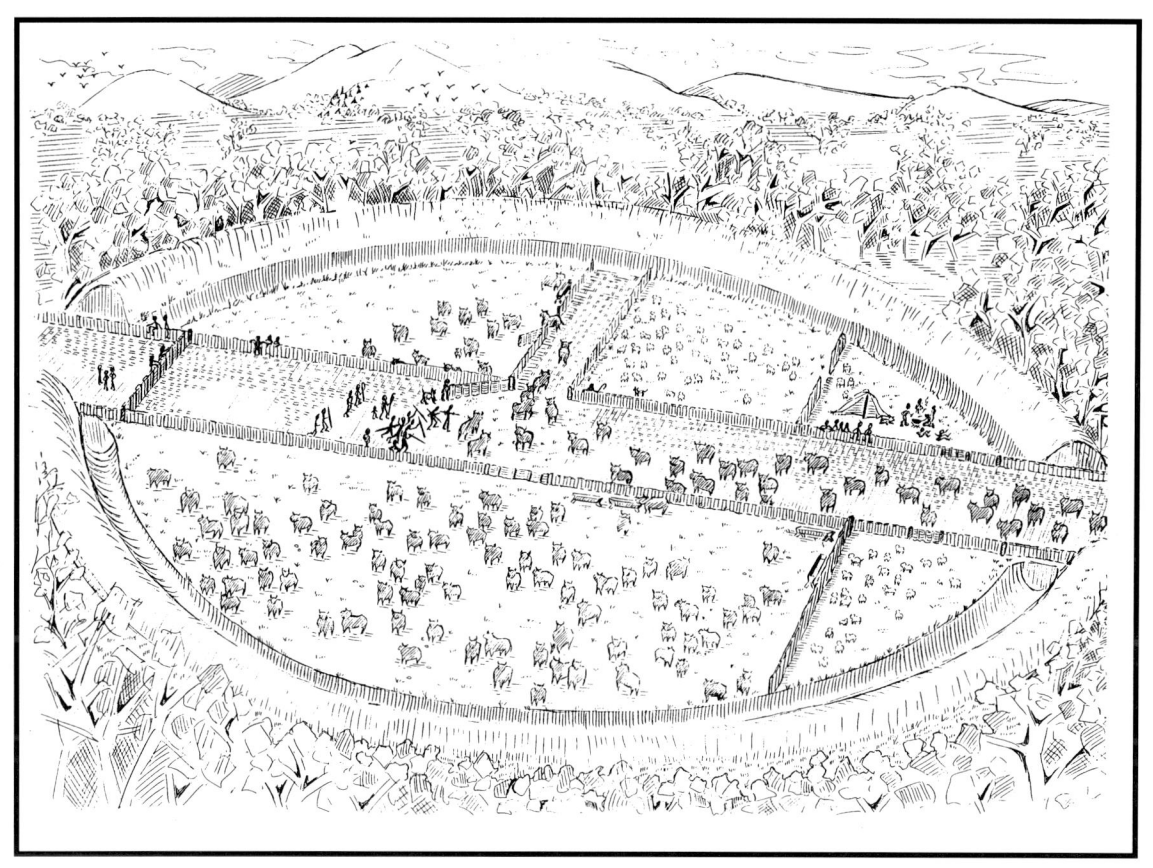

Artist's reconstruction drawing of the henge like enclosure at Milfield which pre-dates Stonehenge by hundreds of years.

the enclosure, were the focus around which the small dispersed settlements were located. Some members of these communities lived in dwellings on the raised gravel terraces of the valley floor, at the excavated sites at Thirlings and Yeavering for example (see map, page 8); settlement sites probably used for short periods but which were returned to again and again during the Neolithic period.

Analysis of sediments has shown that soil degradation during the early Neolithic was avoided, and areas used for small scale horticulture would often be left to regenerate as woodland after a few years of agricultural use. A quernstone (grinding stone) was recovered from the later Neolithic phase of settlement at Thirlings, demonstrating that people were growing grain which was ground into flour, no doubt for bread. Ale was also being produced certainly by the late Neolithic, being associated with, and consumed in, the highly decorated and prestigious Beaker ceramics often found as grave good assemblages in late Neolithic and early Bronze Age burials (see illustration, page 10).

The reduced settlement mobility served to bond particular communities more closely with the territories they occupied. Consequently, this meant exchange between groups which had access to different resources became both necessary and increasingly important. Neutral places where such transactions could take place emerged and are relatively common in southern England where they have survived well; such early Neolithic earthworks with their many entrances being known as causewayed enclosures (banks and ditches made from earth).

The Coupland Enclosure, excavated as part of the author's Milfield Basin Archaeological Landscape Project, to the south of Milfield village (mentioned above) may have served a similar purpose, in addition to its perennial role as a stock compound, providing a place where people could exchange commodities such as flint, leather, pottery, foodstuffs and the highly sought after stone axes. The physical delineation of these places by earthworks positioned the space within these enclosures outside the domain of any particular territory, and created neutral points for inter-group contact. Evidence from elsewhere in Britain shows that mass feasting and the consumption of the choicest beef cuts formed an important element in the activities which took place on such sites. Few such sites were permanently occupied, but were rather used for a few days at certain times of the year as gathering places for the dispersed communities who maintained a broader collective identity with each other, probably based on bonds of kinship and descent, reaffirmed at these sites during the gatherings.

What are cup and ring marks ?

These are carvings in stone consisting of an inner hemispherical depression (the cup) with encircling rings (the ring), often with a duct connecting the cup with the outside of the rings. They were originally carved on bedrock during the early Neolithic and were later incorporated in monuments such as stone circles in the later Neolithic and in burial cairns in the Early Bronze Age.

(picture: cup and ring marked rock on Weetwood Moor)

The excavations at the Coupland Enclosure showed that earlier temporary settlement had taken place on this site, indicating that the construction of the enclosure was the culmination of an already established occupation pattern involving seasonal gatherings at this place.

Flint was imported to the Milfield Basin, from the Durham & Cleveland coast and from Yorkshire, although use of the local cherts and agates continued. Stone axes, mostly made from Langdale tuff from the Lake District, the local whinstone and the greywacke slate of southern Scotland, were used to fell areas of forest to provide temporary clearances for settlement and the horticultural plots in the Early Neolithic. Round-based earthenware pottery, particularly useful for cooking as they spread the heat evenly in the same way as a wok, were produced using local clay from the river Till. A wide range of wooden, leather and bone objects were produced, though few survive because of their poor preservation properties. However, many such artefacts are known from waterlogged environments which do preserve such organic remains, such as the Neolithic finds from Etton, Cambridgeshire or those from Ehenside Tarn in Cumbria for example.

There were probably few divisions between subsistence, ritual, social and political practices during Neolithic times. These aspects of life, which we differentiate between today, were welded together in the activities and fabric of daily life and the seasonal patterns of behaviour.

Artist's recreation of Roughting Lynn, near Milfield,
the site of the largest cup and ring marked outcrop in England.

Early Neolithic arrowheads

  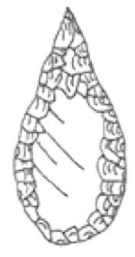  

Later Neolithic-Early Bronze Age Arrowheads

   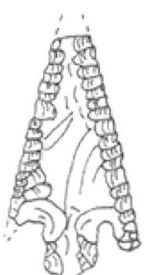 

Cults of the ancestors which involved the construction of large cairns, both long and round, containing the skeletal remains of numerous individuals, also appear to have operated in conjunction with the wielding of social and ritual power and the sanctioning of territorial rights by invoking ancestral rites to an area.

Significant changes took place between 3000 and 2000BC, separating out the Late Neolithic as distinct from the Early Neolithic period - including, most notably, the widespread construction of ritual monuments across whole tracts of landscape. This included the construction of a massive henge complex and the erection of standing stones.

What is a Henge?

A henge is not a stone circle, but rather a circular monument formed by an outer mound and inner ditch with, usually, one or two entrances.

Sometimes there is an inner setting of stone or wooden uprights. They functioned as open air ceremonial monuments where religious rites and possibly the exchange of the highly valued stone-axe took place.

They vary in size from 17m in diameter at Wormy Hillock in Aberdeenshire to 427 m at Avebury in Wiltshire. However, the henges in the Milfield Basin average 25-30m across.

A series of henge monuments, ritual centres - most easily conceived of as open-air temples - and defined by circular earthworks comprising an external bank and internal ditch, were constructed across the Milfield Plain, being deliberately positioned along the axes of the rivers Glen and Till. This is one of the densest complexes of henge monuments known in Britain and emphasises the importance of this sacred landscape as not only the regional centre of Northumberland, but also its wider significance at this time.

One of these ceremonial monuments, that known as Milfield North, was also accompanied by an avenue defined by standing wooden posts, which was possibly used as a processional way by some of the worshippers who used this religious site. Other types of ritual sites were also constructed to provide sacred places for worship and ritual, namely stone circles, such as the ones at Duddo, Doddington Moor and Threestone Burn, in addition to isolated standing stones such as the King's Stone near Pallinsburn, the Bendor Stone near Akeld and the Battle Stone at Yeavering.

The cup mark symbols can be found incorporated into some of these new monuments, such as on the standing stones at the Duddo circle, and one found in a pit at the Milfield South henge.

By 2000BC a new development took place revealed by the occurrence of pit alignments across the Milfield Pain, which archaeologists believe are the traces of ancient field boundaries, especially given the geometric pattern of their layout and the positioning of entrances through these boundaries. These pits have been shown to have held posts which formed the supports either for fences or hedged boundaries. This concept of land tenure, where specific and emphatically demarcated land plots were established, implies the existence of a centralised authority which had the power to instigate and mobilise the labour necessary to create and maintain this new system of land allotment.

The geometric, and thus planned, layout ignored the previous values and rules which had constituted peoples' access to and relationship with the land.

The excavations on the Henge at Milfield North showed that this henge had been oriented so that the view out of its southern entrance was directly aligned on the prominent mountain of Yeavering Bell, suggesting that this imposing eminence had some sacred significance.

Henges elsewhere in Britain are known to have been sited with some astronomical significance in mind, such as at Avebury and Stonehenge for example, and it is likely that the Milfield monuments may also share similar celestial connotations. However, further work is required before this can be established.

These monuments imposed a strictly defined ritual order over the landscape, and as such the belief systems and social order became monumentalized in the landscape in a similar fashion to the way the cup and ring marks on outcrop rock had symbolised the beliefs of earlier communities there.

However, the important difference was that this new ordering of the

What is a Stone Circle ?

A stone circle consists of a ring of standing stones set in a circular, or nearly circular, arrangement. Sometimes such circles were made from timber instead of stone.

Like henges, these probably functioned as open air temples, though they are often associated with astronomical events at certain times of the year (such as mid-winter or, mid-summer sunrise, for example). They are sometimes constructed in henge monuments as at Stonehenge, for example, and as was probably the case at East Marley Knowe in the Milfield Plain. However, they usually occur on their own or associated with stone avenues along which processions of the faithful may have trod.

Artist's reconstruction of Duddo Fourstones stonecircle
with Yeavering Bell and the Cheviots in the background

landscape was much more strictly defined, achieved through the construction of man-made monuments rather than enhanced natural features (as was the case with the rock carvings), resulting in a less ambiguous, and therefore less questionable statement of the social ordering.

Greater control was being wielded over these expanded communities by an emergent elite who exercised their spiritual authority to legitimate and control the new order of social relations that had developed.

The use of visually impressive monuments, and a new system of land division, implies that a new ideological relationship had developed between humans and the natural world. Humans now perceived themselves as active agents involved in controlling the world around them, rather than custodians of their environment. The rituals carried out at these monuments would have embodied these new beliefs. The burial of a cup marked stone slab at Milfield South henge may, indeed, have been the result of a ritual act to bury the old beliefs.

The sudden and dramatic intensification of land use is echoed in the environmental record. Large quantities of sediments were deposited in the flood plain on the valley floor between 2500 and 2000BC. This occurred as a result of soil erosion and rainwater run-off in the uplands, caused by large scale woodland clearance. Pollen evidence has also shown that these upland areas were being cleared for stock grazing and some limited agricultural activities.

Settlement may still have included a certain amount of seasonal mobility though the trend towards permanent settlement was underway, certainly by the Late Neolithic. The population had increased significantly by the end of this period and raw materials such as flint were being imported into the area on a much larger scale than before, and there was less reliance on the poorer quality local lithic materials. These wider-ranging and improved exchange networks indicate that the fragmented communities which had inhabited the Milfield Basin in the early Neolithic were coalescing into larger tribal units which had well developed contacts, and greater interaction with other tribal groups.

This is also made apparent by the widespread use of the highly decorated Grooved Ware pottery which is often found associated with henge monuments. The occurrence of the henge phenomenon throughout the whole of the British Isles is indicative of the capacity of these widely dispersed communities for assimilating ideas gained through the increased levels of contact between groups. Settlement still remained largely as a dispersed pattern across the landscape, although some larger villages may have emerged as is suggested by the enclosed Neolithic site at Meldon Bridge in Peebleshire. However, the remains of any such settlement in the Milfield Basin are likely to be situated in the attractive locations occupied by modern settlements such as Milfield village or Wooler for example, and so we await their discovery.

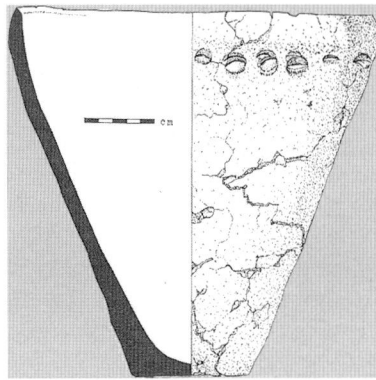

Late Neolithic 'Peterborough Ware' Pot, found at Thirlings, Milfield.

The Ages of Bronze and Iron

The period between 2000BC and the arrival of the Romans in around 80AD witnessed a considerable departure from previous periods in terms of the way people lived, worked and thought. The adoption of new technologies, including the widespread use of metal at the expense of flint, contributed to the processes of social and ideological transformations which allowed change to take place.

Traditional explanations for these changes which invoke migrations and invasions have now been largely abandoned in favour of more complex interconnected processes of social, economic, ideological and environmental change.

The climate remained comparatively warm and stable during the early and mid 2nd millennium BC until a period of climatic deterioration c.1200-800BC. This deterioration may have encouraged some abandonment of settlement in the uplands, which had previously been very heavily deforested and colonised by farming communities during the preceding centuries of the Bronze Age. As intensive farming since then has never reached the altitudinal limits achieved during the 2nd millennium BC, many of the remains of these settlements and their associated field systems and paddocks remain fossilized in the landscape and are still visible as low grass covered earthworks, often above the 300m contour.

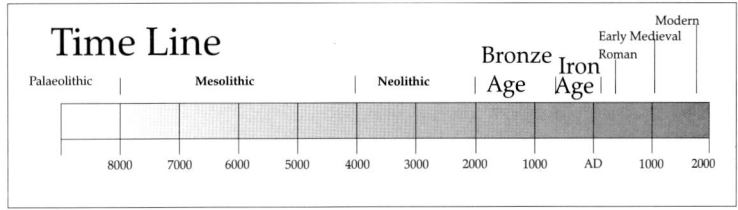

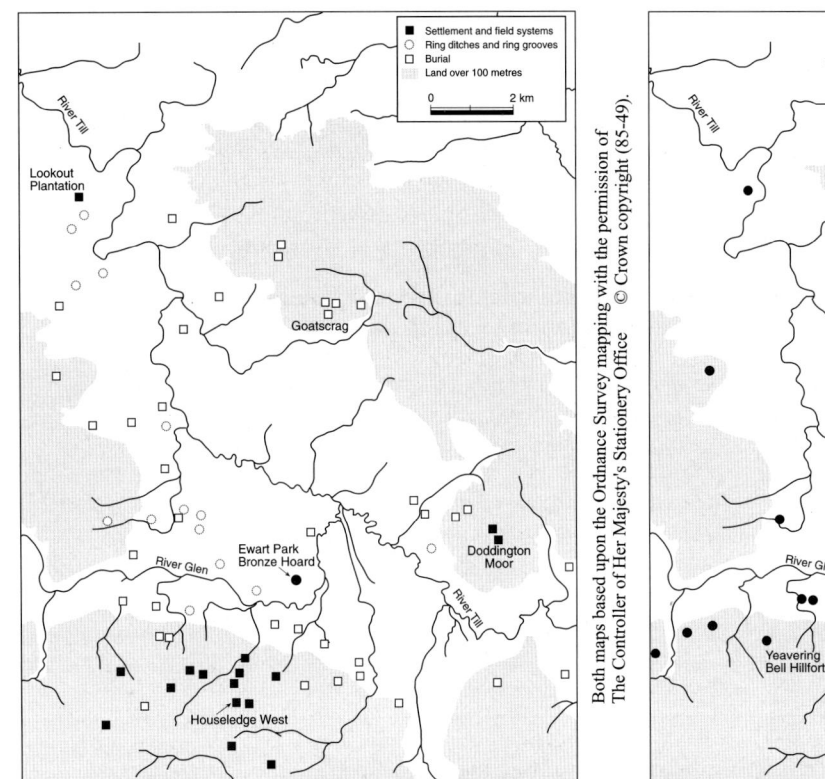

Early Bronze Age sites in the Milfield Basin

Iron Age and Romano-British sites in the Milfield Basin

The legacy of this mass woodland clearance in the uplands is the barren open moorland landscapes which predominate today.

This early period of the Bronze Age not only saw the extension of farming into the uplands, but the establishment of farming in a way with which we are more familiar today. Farming appears to have become a more secularised activity less, though not fully, divorced from the ritual aspects of life which had previously formed a more integral part of land-use strategies. With new technologies came an increase in task specialisation, and the emergence of specific occupations and roles within society which can be recognised by the latter part of the 2nd millennium BC.

Metal smiths, potters, farmers, a nobility, a warrior class, a religious class, and possibly even slaves, meant not only demarcation of roles within society whereby people became more reliant on group co-operation, but also enhanced social differentiation, access to wealth and power, and a differential quality of life for people of varying social status. The symbolic divisions of the landscape that had existed in previous periods had finally given way to more unequivocal boundary markers in the form of extensive land boundaries which by now extended over the uplands and can still be discerned today as low turf covered walls and dykes, often extending for several kilometres.

These upland farmsteads consisted of circular buildings, usually with stone footings, though sometimes made with wooden uprights, set into the hillside in artificially levelled scoops, many of which can be seen in the Cheviot Hills on the south side of the Milfield Basin. The plots associated with these houses average 0.2ha. in extent and are usually irregular or curvilinear in plan. Stone clearance indicates that this was impoved land, possibly used for cultivation, while livestock remained the mainstay of the economy. At Hallshill, Redesdale, houses yielded remains of wheat, barley, oats, flax and agricultural weeds, providing an insight into the type of crops harvested by these hill farmers. Excavations at Houseledge, Black Law, to the south of Yeavering Bell, revealed a succession of three buildings on this site, as well as stock pens and burial cairns associated with the settlement. Clearance cairns are a common feature associated with these upland settlements, resulting from the clearance of stone off land destined for improvement to farmland.

The settlement evidence for the valley floor does, however, remain meagre due, most probably, to the intensive land-use throughout the last few thousand years which has both eradicated and masked much of the archaeological evidence that was not of a monumental nature. However, it is likely that settlement and farming (whether pastoral or arable) continued on much of the valley floor from the beginning of the 2nd millennium through until the present, although some archaeologists have suggested the Milfield Plain was abandoned c.2000-1200BC due to social and economic collapse and population decline. However, the excavation and secure dating of a Bronze Age settlement at Lookout Plantation near Crookham on the valley floor makes this unlikely.

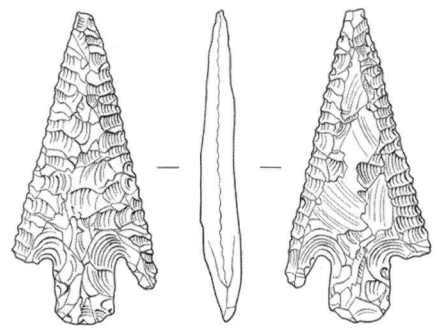

Early Bronze Age arrowhead found to the west of Milfield village

Intensive farming in the Till Valley has made recognition of past settlement difficult. For early periods, the use of stone tools means there is a certain amount of durable evidence that can still be found, but for later periods it is more difficult to pinpoint occupation sites in the plain. This lack of readily observable evidence is not, however, evidence of abandonment but rather a product of subsequent intensive land use. It is only for the Anglo-Saxon period that settlements can be easily recognised (from aerial photographs which show discolorations in crops and soil where they overlie structures), and this is probably due to the particular construction techniques used during this period.

The Bronze Age witnessed a move towards cremation as the main form of mortuary rite rather than inhumation, which had tended to dominate in burials of the previous period. Burials were made singly in a diverse range of circular burial monuments which include cairns of various constructional styles, such as those which can be found on Chatton Sandyford Moor for example, and flat cremation cemeteries enclosed by a circular ditch (such as the one excavated at the base of Whitton Hill, Milfield).

These burials were often contained in special cremation pots (cinerary urns and 'food vessels'- names given to these pots by early antiquaries), of which food vessels and collared urns are the most common types. This trend of burying individuals in their own specific graves, often with a selection of prestigious grave goods, reflects a greater concern with the importance of certain individuals in society as well as more overt hierarchisation and segregation between people of different status. Clearly, most people did not receive this type of burial, it being reserved for selected members of society only. This marks an important difference from the Neolithic practice of communal burials in a single monument.

Occasional finds of Bronze artefacts, including much weaponry, have been recovered from the Milfield Plain, such as the assemblages from Ewart and Coupland, dating to the early 1st millennium BC.

The evidence for increasing insecurity and warfare by 800BC, if not before, is also confirmed by the construction of enclosed palisaded settlements at this time. Excavations on the defended farmstead at Fenton Hill on the east side of the river Till have shown that this site was defended by a part single, part double stockade, constructed about 800BC. By the late 2nd and early 1st millennium BC a political and social organization had emerged capable of long-term planning, mobilising large labour forces, constructing large enclosures and controlling the division of land and territories. The population at the end of the Bronze Age had increased, no doubt adding to pressures on both land and resources,

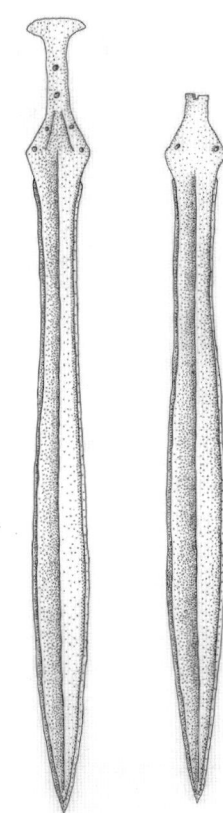

Bronze Age Swords found Ewart Park, Nr. Milfield

and it is under such conditions that the development of a settlement hierarchy of defended sites had its origins. By the mid-first millennium BC more prominent defences were constructed, such as the hillfort on Dod Law and the many other well-preserved forts which dot the sandstone escarpment and Cheviot Hills. These massive hillforts, with stone and earth ramparts often accompanied by rock-cut ditches, serve to reinforce the impression of the increasingly warlike nature of society at this time. The large number of hut stances for stone and timber buildings that can be seen in the massive hillfort on Yeavering Bell for example, demonstrate that some of these forts, at least, were not just citadels occupied during emergencies, but rather permanently occupied defended villages or small townships.

The fortress on Yeavering Bell is the largest and most densely occupied English hillfort north of Yorkshire, and is thought to be the capital from which the tribal area of Northumberland was governed. This previously sacred mountain seems to have been appropriated for use as the political centre of the tribal kingdom of the Iron Age.

An Iron Age wheel from Ryton, Tynedale
(Courtesy, Museum of Antiquities, Newcastle upon Tyne)

Cattle provided the mainstay of the economy, although the keeping of sheep, pigs and horses and the production of grain would have been other important elements. The horse became an important animal for the warrior elites of the Iron Age communities, giving them not only added mobility and advantage in battle, but also an important means for demonstrating prestige and power.

A new type of cultivation came into being during the Iron Age of the borders region known as cord rigg (see page 29), consisting of narrow riggs, low ridges about 1m wide, similar in form to lazy beds. Remains of these old cultivation surfaces can be seen in the Cheviot Hills around many of the enclosed settlements which date to this period. The use of the iron plough probably had an important role in bringing about this innovation in farming techniques which helped keep temperatures up in the rigg while encouraging drainage in the furrows between, the net result being greater productivity and the expansion of agriculture into upland areas.

There is little evidence of how the dead were disposed of in the Iron Age, though it is likely that cremation continued as the principal mortuary rite. That ritual remained strong is not in doubt, as Caesar refers at length to the power and influence of the Druids after his short lived invasion in 55-54BC. Natural places such as groves, springs and lakes were the sacred places used by these mystics to perform their rites, and thus it is not surprising that there is very little visible archaeological evidence of their activities. However, their fascination with skulls and votive offerings, particularly in water, provides possibilities for archaeological discoveries. Furthermore, an unusual structure on the east summit within Yeavering Bell hillfort could very well be a druidic temple, though this can only be confirmed by excavation.

Early Bronze Age Food Vessel Ford

Early Bronze Age Urn from a barrow at Ford

Bronze or Iron Age gold chain from Flodden area (Courtesy, Alnwick Castle Museum)

The Romano-British Period

North Northumberland lies to the north of Hadrian's Wall and therefore the evidence for the Romano-British period is not as stunning as the famous frontier zone to the south. Although the Roman occupations and incursions north of the wall were sporadic and shortlived they form a fascinating tale which is the subject of another, more detailed, story which can only be recounted here in brief.

When the Roman emperor Claudius was able to land his forces in Britain in 43AD, eleven of the British tribes did not oppose the Roman presence, which was initially aimed at the conquest of southern England, and the wresting of power from the powerful Catuvelluani tribe.

The growing strength and influence of the Catuvelluani tribe was causing concern to many other British tribes at this time and these internal jealousies and political wrangles handed the invading Roman forces a useful situation to exploit, whereby tribes could be isolated and picked off one by one. The tribes of northern England and southern Scotland were at first prepared to capitulate to the Romans. However, when the Brigantian queen, Cartimandua, was forced out by her ex-husband Venutias, the kingdom of Brigantia took on the Roman legions. Ultimately Brigantia, the land between the river Trent to the south and the rivers Tyne and Solway to the north, fell to Roman rule in 78AD, and the neutral Votadini tribe, which inhabited Northumberland, including the Milfield Basin and eastern parts of southern Scotland, almost certainly became a client kingdom of Rome- a relationship which would have required them to pay tribute.

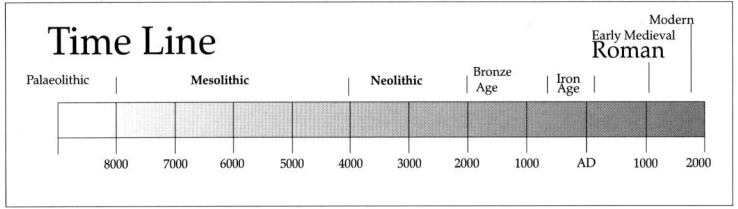

When the Roman general Agricola campaigned into Scotland in 81AD roads leading north were constructed to facilitate rapid movement of troops and supplies. The Roman road known as **The Devils Causeway** (see map, page 22) was built through the Votadini territory linking Dere Street, just north of the Roman fort at Corbridge, with Berwick. This road skirts the east side of the sandstone escarpment fringing the Milfield Plain, and the modern road from East Horton to Lowick follows its line for most of its course.

This area was occupied by Rome until the end of the 1st century AD before they withdrew to the Tyne-Solway isthmus. From then on the kingdom of the Votadini, probably now centred on the great hillfort at Traprain Law in the East Lothians of south-east Scotland, was for most of the Romano-British period a client kingdom of the Roman empire, although later Roman advances during the Antonine and Severan periods may have reincorporated this region into the empire, though only for short periods.

The impact of the Romans on north Northumberland probably had a greater effect on the elite and ruling classes than on the ordinary folk. The elite would, no doubt, have had access to Roman luxury goods such as jewellery, wine and fine pottery for example, but otherwise there is very little evidence that even the privileged classes became Romanized like the elites in southern England who learnt Latin, lived in villas and were encouraged to emulate the architecture and lifestyles of the Mediterranean world.

What is Cord Rigg?

Cord Rigg is the name given to a form of arable farming, first recognised in the Borders, which was in use from at least the Iron Age and into the Romano-British period. It consists of ridges (riggs) separated by furrows. The ridges are rarely more than 1m wide and are now low in height, making them most clearly visible in low sunlight or under a light snow covering.

Piling up earth into riggs helps raise the temperature, and protects newly sown crops from frost damage, as well as ensuring good drainage into the furrows either side. Examples are best preserved in the Cheviot uplands such as those above Ingram on Wether Hill.

Continuity in settlement patterns and land-use can be traced from the Pre-Roman Iron Age and into the Romano-British period, with the farmsteads in their curvilinear or irregular compounds still visible on the ground in the Cheviot Hills fringing the Milfield Plain. People were still using the same sort of material culture (artefacts) as in the Iron Age, with pottery, querns, beads, bangles and brooches the more common finds on such sites. Excavations at these settlement sites has shown that although the later Romano-British phases were constructed in stone, they usually replaced timber farmsteads which had occupied these sites from at least the 2nd and 1st centuries BC, such as occurred at the site at Hetha Burn in the College Valley at the west end of the Milfield Basin. In addition, the site at Hetha Burn was ultimately expanded from a farmstead in the early Romano-British period with two buildings, into a hamlet with ten round stone buildings by the 2nd century AD.

The vast number of these Romano-British sites now recognised throughout Northumberland are testament to the rising population during the first two centuries AD and the massive clearances for grazing which continued to take place in the uplands.

Pollen diagrams from peat bogs adjacent to the Milfield Basin at Camp Hill Moss and Steng Moss show that agriculture remained important with grain, including wheat, and more particularly barley, being commonly grown. The barley was used for both human consumption and as animal feed, as well as for brewing ale. However, stock rearing, particularly cattle, but also horses, remained dominant and took place both in the uplands and on parts of the valley floor. The agriculture, where it took place, was situated on the attractive free-draining areas of the valley floors, as well as on suitable areas of upland where cord-rigg cultivation continued. The intensification of farming in the 1st and 2nd centuries AD may reflect the pressure put on the Votadini by the Romans to provide tribute by way of food levies. The collection of stock and grain was undertaken by the existing ruling elite who then passed this on to the Romans in order to secure their independence and maintain their position as a client kingdom.

The evidence for settlement from the 3rd century AD until the Early Medieval period is difficult to detect in the archaeological record. This is in part due to a lack of fieldwork and also the invisibility of this period in terms of well preserved archaeological remains. It is thought, however, that the population levels also experienced a decline during these years, possibly brought about by deliberate depopulation of this frontier zone by Septimius Severus

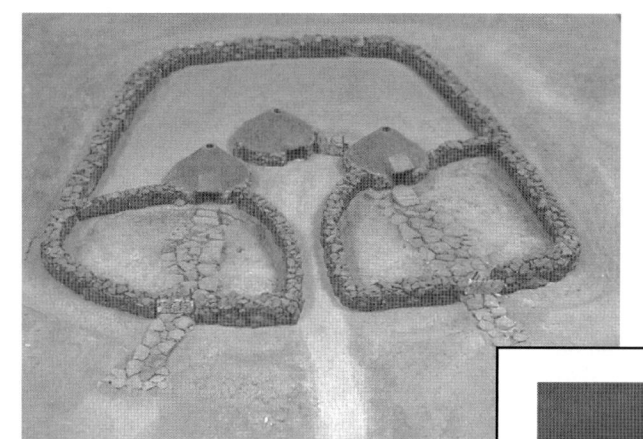

Model of enclosed Romano-British farmstead excavated at Riding Wood, North Tynedale
(Photo courtesy of the Museum of Antiquities, Newcastle upon Tyne)

Reconstructed model of the Romano-British farmstead at Huckhoe, showing the internal structure.
(Photo courtesy of the Museum of Antiquities, Newcastle upon Tyne)

*T*he Cheviot Hills, to the south and west of the Milfield Plain, contain one of the richest areas of Iron Age and Romano-British remains in England. Within this upland massif are vast numbers of hill forts, enclosed farmsteads, cord rigg and land boundaries. Given the wealth of archaeology in the area they have, as yet, experienced relatively little investigation.

and subsequently Caracalla in the 3rd century AD as a way of securing peace in the frontier zone. The mass acquisition of young men as recruits to fight for the Roman army on its far flung frontiers of empire is a likely cause of this depopulation, a process which must have caused great distress among the community in the Milfield area.

Little is known of Iron Age and Romano-British burial and ritual practices as they have left very little archaeological trace. However, accounts by Roman writers indicate that the Druids wielded great power within society. Although the power base of the Druids was finally broken by the Roman attack on one of their great centres, on Anglesey, in 60AD, local deities continued to be revered and propitiated, with water offerings still common. Religion remained polytheistic whereby a variety of godheads and deities were embraced in the religious observances of any one tribe. Disposal of the dead may have been largely by cremation and subsequent scattering of ashes. However, higher status individuals were probably buried in their own graves or buried in already existing burial mounds constructed in earlier periods, as was the case with the 3rd century AD burial in an earlier cairn on Chatton Sandyford Moor on the south-east side of the Milfield Basin, which was found to be accompanied by a decorated pottery drinking flagon of this period.

By the late 4th century incursions by Picts and Scots into northern Britain, and the final abandonment of Britain by the Romans and the ruling elites by 410AD, resulted in a power vacuum being created. This led to serious instability in most northern communities upsetting the political, social and economic balance and exposing communities wholesale to war, pillage and rape. The withdrawal of the Romans and the existing ruling classes of many of the British tribes created an anarchic situation, particularly in the north, which, accompanied by famine, lead to brigandage and a collapse in food production. Excavations in the 19th century have shown that the Iron Age hillfort at Yeavering Bell was reoccupied in the late 4th century, and no doubt served as the seat of governance in this time of crisis when defence and warfare once again became a primary concern. Adverse conditions indeed, and a time, if ever one was needed, for heroes!

The Early Medieval Period

With the departure of the ruling and military elite, the northern communities were left to organise their own resistance. This situation gave rise to the emergence of small polities (political units) often based around single valley communities governed by a warrior-leader and his warband.

These tyrannies, as the monk Gildas called them, were ubiquitous throughout northern Britain, and although civil war among the British tyrants was endemic, they were eventually successful in driving out the Scots and Picts. The communities supporting these ruling tyrants could only supply them with staples such as food, horses and basic materials, while access to wealth, power and therefore, ultimately, a measure of security and stability, was only gained by raiding for booty, slaves and cattle. The initial disorder in the early decades of the 5th century eventually gave way to a more stable environment, which although still violent and susceptible to constant and sudden changes in the ruling factions, allowed for the revitalisation of local economies and the farming base on which the ordinary person relied.

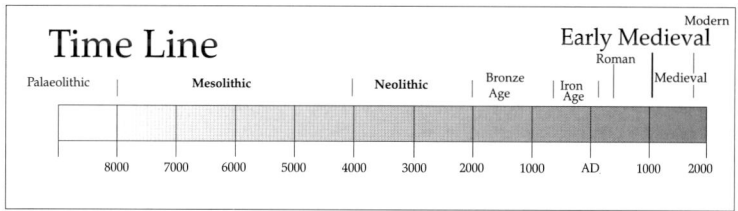

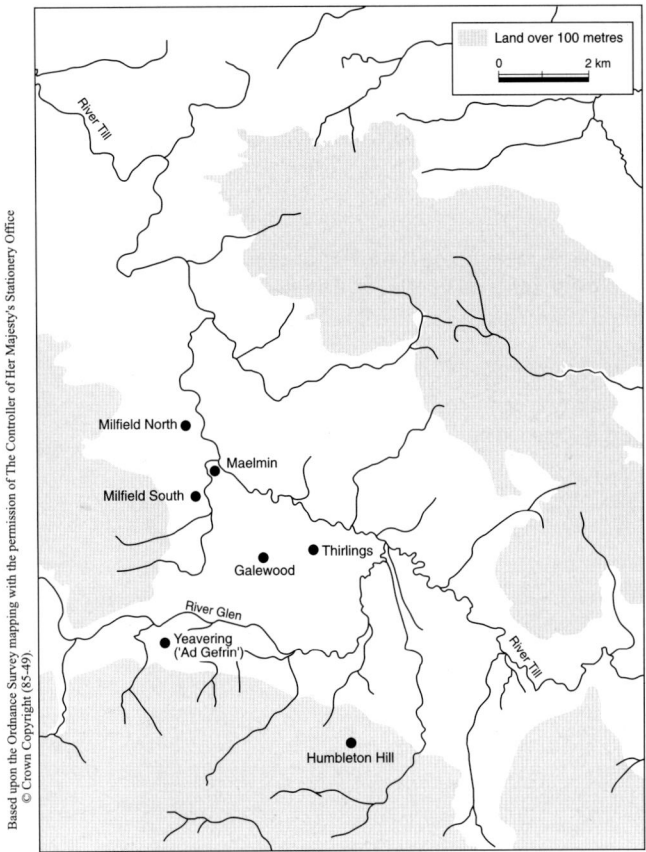

Archaeological sites of the early Medieval Period

King Arthur

There existed almost a century of relative peace between c.450AD and 540AD, which is the period within which the heroic **King Arthur** of legend is said to have lived. The important references to Arthur made by the 9th century monk, Nennius, states that Arthur fought a series of twelve victorious battles in which he triumphed over the enemies of the British during the 490s AD. It is important to note that Nennius records that "The first battle was at the mouth of the river Glein", and although there are a number of river Glens in Britain, it is likely that this could refer to the river Glen in the Milfield Basin, particularly as the important Anglo-British palace site of Yeavering is located at the mouth of the Glen valley, as the passage specifies, and is a strategic site which has witnessed many other battles over the centuries. A number of historians have made the case for Arthur being a war leader based in northern England, and if this is the case, the possible presence of this heroic figure in the vital strategic area of the Milfield Basin, which controls communications both north-south and east-west, comes as no surprise.

The dynasties which ruled during these middle years of the 1st millennium AD usually enjoyed only short-lived dominance and these small kingdoms were subject to frequent boundary changes and changes in allegiance.

The economy of north Northumberland remained devoid of coinage in the years after 410AD, although very little in the way of a cash economy had existed in Northumberland during the Roman period when most transactions were settled by barter, exchange and payment in kind. A sustained period of prosperity took place in the late 5th century and early 6th century. Widespread grazing and agriculture took hold and the level of forest clearance was maintained, with pastoralism once again the mainstay of the economy, with a strong bias in favour of cattle rearing. Sudden episodes of population decline were experienced, brought about not only by raids and times of war, but more devastatingly by pestilence. Several outbreaks of plague are known to have affected the north including ones in the mid 6th century, the late 7th century and in the early 8th century.

Little is known of the settlements of this period, although continuity in the location and form of rural farmsteads is evidenced at Yeavering, where a Romano-British occupation was believed by the excavator to have been succeeded by an early British settlement on the same site. However, the central places from which the early tyrants and later dynastic rulers wielded power were probably re-fortified Iron Age hillforts, which saw a heavy investment in new defences to create very strongly defended hilltop citadels.

The Milfield Basin and the rest of north Northumberland was probably ruled at this time from the citadel on Humbleton Hill which is prominently located between the modern town of Wooler and Yeavering Bell, which a recent survey has shown has at least two phases of construction, the second being a massive strengthening and reorganisation of the defences including the construction of additional massive dry-stone ramparts.

The mid-6th century witnessed the conquest of what is now modern Northumberland by an Anglian king and his sons and the displacement of the previous elite. However, this did not bring a colonisation of the north by Anglo-Saxons, but rather a new royal line and warrior class which no doubt attracted to itself many of the existing British warrior class who would be attracted by the patronage which successful warrior kings could offer. This king, Ida, and his sons Theodric and Adda, who may have travelled north from Yorkshire, were responsible for carving out the kingdom of Bernicia (a British tribal name meaning people of the mountain passes) which extended over the modern area of Northumberland and south-east Scotland. Ida landed at Bamburgh and completed his conquest from this commanding strategic location. He set up two capitals, or royal vills, from which to rule this kingdom, one at Bamburgh and the other at Yeavering in the Milfield Plain. The British rather than later Anglian names for Yeavering (Ad Gefrin), Bamburgh (Dingaray), the river Glen (Glin), in addition to the tribal name Bernicia were retained by these early Anglian kings, probably in a show of respect for the historic significance of these places to the British population, thus helping to legitimate their claims and merge their dynastic line with the fortunes of the kingdom by modelling themselves as its true heirs. At the same time, these kings also gave their names to new settlements, such as Adderstone to the west of Bamburgh, meaning the settlement of Adda. This new and enlarged kingdom quickly became very strong and posed a serious threat to all the surrounding powers who felt the need to join forces and contain the rise of this kingdom. A series of battles against the powerful Urien, king of what is now North Yorkshire and Cumbria (Catraeth and Rheged respectively), by Theodric and subsequently Adda, resulted ultimately in the loss of Urien's kingdom to Bernicia shortly after Urien's death.

A federation of British and Welsh kingdoms to the south and west of Bernicia together with the Scots and Picts to the north attempted to strike a mortal blow to the Bernician kingdom, but this resulted in a catastrophic defeat for this confederation at the battle of Catraeth (modern Catterick in North Yorkshire), the account of this tragedy being remembered in the poem known as The Goddodin. The Anglian kingdoms of Bernicia, and Deira to the south, were united around 600AD by the Bernician king Aethelfrith, giving rise to the enlarged kingdom which then became known as Northumbria, that is, the lands north of the Humber. This new kingdom extended from the area of the river Trent to the south northwards into what is now southern Scotland, including the areas on both sides of the Pennines.

The Scots, Picts and Irish again attacked Northumbria from the north in 603AD but this resulted in a heavy defeat for the invaders at the battle of Degastan. The kingdom of Goddodin, and its capital Edinburgh, fell to Northumberland around 638AD. By this time Northumbria covered all lands from roughly the Trent to the Forth, as well as the Isle of Man. Attacks on the Scots, Ireland and Anglesey are indicative of the expansionist aims of the warrior kings at this time. However, clashes with kingdoms to the south by the mid 7th century, due to Northumbrian ambitions south of the Humber in Lindsey (Lincolnshire) and Wales, met with less success. Defeat in 633 against the forces of Penda of Mercia and Cadwallon of Gwynedd for the Northumbrian king Edwin at Hadfield cost the northern king his life. Edwin's successor, Oswald, defeated Cadwallon's forces at the battle of Hexham in 634, where Cadwallon himself was killed. Oswald, however, also died in battle against the Mercian forces of Penda at Maserfelth in 642. Ultimately though, Oswy secured the Northumbrian kingdom against the Mercians and their Welsh allies by a decisive victory over Penda in 657, during which Penda was killed.

The political and military ascendency of Northumbria suffered a setback in the north by the Pictish victory at Nechtansmere in 685. Although, shortly after, Ecgfrith reasserted Northumbrian authority in the north with successful raids on Ireland and Dalriada and in the south by the temporary annexation of Lindsey (modern Lincolnshire).

The limits of Northumbrian expansion had been reached and in the following centuries the gradual erosion of Northumbrian authority took place. However, although the 8th century was dominated by internal power struggles, Northumbria's boundaries remained relatively secure and this enabled a flowering of Northumbrian culture and learning. This period saw such great works as the Lindisfarne Gospels, the writings of the monk Bede, the creation of many monastic centres of learning such as Monkwearmouth, Jarrow, Lindisfarne and Hexham and the flourishing of stone sculpture and masonry skills employed on the stone churches of the time.

Yeavering

Until c.685 the royal seat at Yeavering with its great halls, open air auditorium, massive defended enclosure, temple and ancillary buildings, was one of the principal places from which the kingdom of Northumbria was governed. Kingship was peripatetic, which meant that the king and his retinue were constantly moving between royal palaces where the surpluses were collected and consumed, order maintained, justice dispensed and laws proclaimed.

Maelmin

After Edwin's and Oswald's defeats at the hands of Penda and Cadwallon, the royal palace at Yeavering was moved a couple of miles northwards to Maelmin, that is, modern Milfield, to control the main crossing of the Till, and no doubt to establish a new site which did not carry the memories of defeat, as Yeavering had been sacked and burnt on both occasions by Penda and Cadwallon. However importance was still attached to the Milfield Basin by succeeding Northumbrian kings as is testified by the relocation of this royal site at Milfield, which lies at the very heart of the Milfield Plain. The extensive remains of Maelmin lie buried under the plough soil in the large fields between the modern village and the river Till, being easily discernible on aerial photographs.

Detail from reconstruction drawing opposite, showing housing and auditorium. (Copyright English Heritage)

The buildings at the high status sites of Yeavering and Maelmin were constructed of wood and were rectangular in shape. They included large halls in which up to about 300 people could be seated and fed, as well as small buildings used for living quarters, workshops and stables. The lower status sites in the valley, the farmsteads and hamlets of the ordinary folk, were also rectangular and constructed of wood, but were smaller and more crudely built. These small houses are known as *Grubenhäuser* and examples of such sites have been excavated at Thirlings and at New Bewick, both on gravel terraces adjacent to the river Till.

The use of stone for building did, however, continue in areas where stone was readily available as a building material. In the hills, the small rectangular shepherds huts known as shielings were constructed and used as part of a transhumance farming strategy by which summer grazing took place on the upland fells and winter pasture was confined to the lowlands.

Intensive land-use continued with St. Cuthbert being known to have grown barley on the nearby Farne Islands, and farming communities who reared cattle resided at the farm complex at Greenshiel on Lindisfarne where archaeologists have recently uncovered a stone built farmstead consisting of 3 buildings located around a central yard, with a cattle byre and ancillary buildings beyond.

Reconstruction drawing of Yeavering AD 627 by Peter Dunn. (Copyright English Heritage)

Paganism

The long standing inhabitants of north Northumberland whose ancestors had lived there for hundreds, if not thousands, of years remained largely pagan, even though Christianity had been preached in parts of Northumbria as early as the 5th century when St. Ninian preached the celtic brand of Christianity from his Northumbrian monastic base at Whithorn in what is now Galloway. However, the fiercely pagan early Anglian kings prompted the later Christian monk, Simeon of Durham, to comment unfavourably on these warlords in an attempt to defile their names for posterity. For example, he libellously remarks of Adda that he was cast into the lower regions, as he deserved.

A bronze 'hanging bowl' from Capheaton, probably dating from the 7th century AD.
(Courtesy of the Museum of Antiquities, Newcastle upon Tyne)

Excavations at Yeavering revealed a rectangular pagan temple where cattle skulls appeared prominently in the ritual there. Intricately decorated hanging bowls (cauldrons) of precious and semi-precious metals were also an important feature in religious observance, possibly as receptacles for a sacred drink, such as wine, which was consumed by devotees. Burials of the early Anglian elites at Yeavering, Galewood and in the henges at Milfield North and Milfield South are not classic Anglo-Saxon burials as are found elsewhere such as in Yorkshire for example, but rather hybridized burials showing both Anglian and Britonic traditions, which adds to the notion of assimilation by the early Anglian elite of Bernicia.

Christianity

Without the support and patronage of the King, Christianity could not flourish, and consequently Northumberland remained strongly pagan until the reign of Edwin who, partly as a political arrangement, married the daughter of the king of Kent, a strongly Christian royal family who probably made Edwin's conversion a condition of marriage. The consequence was that Edwin adopted Christianity, if only in name, and the bishop Paulinus came to Northumberland in 627 and spent 36 days baptising Northumbrians, by full submersion, in the river Glen next to Edwin's palace at Yeavering, where the temple with the cattle skulls was converted into a Christian chapel (see illustration, page 39). It is no accident that this place was chosen for this pivotal and historic event, the Christianisation of Northumberland, as it was an ancient holy centre that had been of great religious significance since at least the late Neolithic when a henge was constructed there.

A 9th century AD Anglo-Saxon cross shaft from Alnmouth depicting the crucifixion. (Courtesy of the Museum of Antiquities, Newcastle upon Tyne)

It seems this sacred place, situated in the lee of a once sacred mountain top (Yeavering Bell), on which an earlier henge was aligned, was selected in preference to anywhere else between the Trent and the Forth due to its recognition as the sacred centre of Northumbria. The location of this momentous event at this symbolic site was reinforced by the use of the river Glen to baptize people, a river along whose course a series of earlier henges and standing stones had been placed, and which no doubt carried sacred connotations itself, given the preoccupation of Britonic pagans with water deities and votive offerings.

Recalling the Arthurian legend of the Lady of the Lake, it is tempting to visualise Excalibur being tossed into the Glen and being caught by the outstretched arm of a goddess. The enchanting landscape of the Milfield Basin clearly contains many more mysteries awaiting discovery!

From the 8th century onwards Northumbria's military and political power was suppressed due mostly to constant internecine warfare usually involving feuds between the leading elites to seize the throne. Kings could not hold the throne for long due to their declining ability to command the wealth and land necessary to maintain a sufficiently large and high quality warrior elite. An important factor in the reduction of kingly wealth and land assets available to reward a warrior class was the fast growing estates of the church whose lands did not return to the king for reallocation on the death of the church incumbent.

The first recorded Viking raid on Northumberland was that on the Lindisfarne monastery in 793, after which further raids on these undefended religious sites, with their civilian population and rich pickings, took place. During a period of civil war Northumberland fell to the Danes in 867. During the early years of the 10th century the English kings managed to re-establish their control in Northumberland. However, after the battle of Brunanburgh in 937, which saw the triumph of the English Saxon kingdoms over a confederacy of Scots, Strathclyde and the Dublin Norse, the modern kingdom known as England was effectively created and the area of Northumberland became an earldom, which ultimately came to be ruled from Alnwick.

Important Events in the Milfield Basin since the Anglian Period

A series of important events, particularly military conflicts, took place in the Milfield Basin in subsequent centuries which had far reaching effects on the course of British history. A few such events are mentioned below.

In 1402 the Earl of Douglas and his Scottish host laid Northumberland waste in response to English incursions into Scottish territory. However, his force, numbering about 10,000 men, was intercepted by the Earl of March, the Duke of Northumberland and his son Harry Hotspur Percy just outside Wooler on the slopes of Humbleton Hill. The English longbow secured an English victory and Douglas, together with many of his knights were captured. It was the subsequent acquaintance of these nobles, and Northumberland's reluctance to pass these prisoners on to the king, Henry IV, which led to the joint attempt by Northumberland, Hotspur and Douglas at overthrowing the king and siezing the throne. It is this failed attempt, in which Hotspur lost his life, that is recorded in Shakespeare's Henry IV Part I.

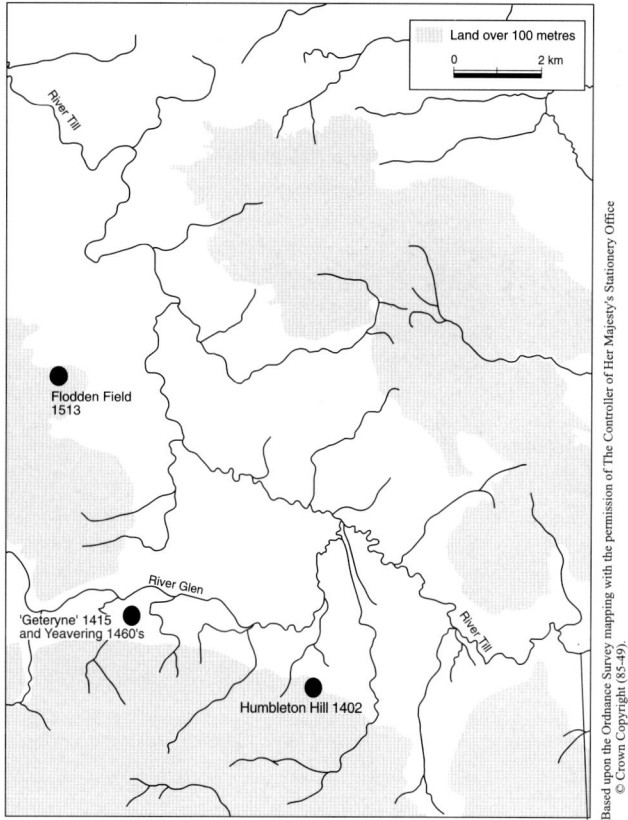

Four main historic battle sites in the Milfield Basin

In 1415 at the battle of Geteryne (Yeavering) Robert Umfraville routed a Scottish force.

An important skirmish in the Wars of the Roses in the mid-1460s also took place in the vicinity of Yeavering, resulting in an important Yorkist victory which paved the way for the establishment of Yorkist supremacy achieved at the battle of Hexham which was fought shortly after.

However, probably the most famous military action which took place in the Basin in recorded history is the battle of Flodden Field which took place on the 9th September 1513. This pivotal battle between the Scots under their king, James IV, and the English, under Thomas Howard Earl of Surrey, ended in a crushing Scottish defeat in which many thousands lost their lives. The Scots took up position on Branxton Hill to the west of Milfield, allowing the English to cross the Till unopposed by the Twizel bridge to the north. The battle started with artillery bombardments before the serious hand-to-hand fighting took place. By the late afternoon the battle had been won and James IV and the flower of his nobility lay dead on the field of battle. Today, cannon balls and other relics of this past tragedy continue to be uncovered.

The Milfield Archaeological Landscape Project is a research project aimed at achieving a holistic understanding of the history of this area. Until the last few decades the importance of this forgotten landscape had been largely unrecognised and ignored.

During prehistory this area constituted one of the core areas of human activity in northern Britain. Then, as a place from where the old kings of Northumbria ruled over what is now northern England and southern Scotland the Christianisation of the north took place. As the scene also for pivotal historic battles, this rich landscape is a national archaeological asset.

If you have found any archaeological remains in the Milfield area please contact Clive Waddington at the Department of Geography, Daysh Building, University of Newcastle upon Tyne, NE1 7RU. Examination of finds will help the research - all finds will be returned.

With thanks to:-

Sandra Rowntree for the reconstruction drawings
the many volunteers who have worked on the project (in all weathers)
the landowners and farmers for giving access to their land
Peter and Amanda for hot food and drink
the family of the late Prof. G Jobey for their permission to reproduce the Beaker drawing on page 10

(Drawings on page 27 are taken from 'British Barrows' 1877 by W Greenwell)

Places to Visit

Bamburgh	NU183351
Berwick Museum	Town Centre
Chillingham Castle	NU062259
Doddington Moor-footpath starts at	NT000324
Etal Castle	NT925393
Fenton Hill defended farmstead	NT979354
Flodden Battlefield	NT890372
Goatscrag & Broomridge-footpath starts at	NT982369
Humbleton Hill Hillfort	NT967283
Milfield Country Café Archaeological Display	NT935338
Museum of Antiquities, Newcastle upon Tyne	
Northumberland National Park Visitor Centre (Ingram)	NU019163
Old Bewick (carved rocks, cairns and hillforts)	NT070218
Roughting Lynn	NT983367
Yeavering Bell - footpath around starts at	NT928293
Site of Yeavering Anglo-Saxon Palace & Fort	NT927305

Useful Maps

1:50,000 (Ordnance Survey ' Landranger' series) No.75 Berwick-upon-Tweed and No. 81 Alnwick, Morpeth and surrounding area.
1:25,000(Ordnance Survey 'Pathfinder' series) No.463 Coldstream. No.464 Lowick. No.475 Wooler

Further Reading

Campbell, J (ed.) 1991 The Anglo-Saxons	Penguin	ISBN 0 14 014395 5
Darvill, T. 1988 Prehistoric Britain	Batsford	ISBN 0 7134 51807
Higham, N. 1986 The Northern Counties to AD1000	Longman	ISBN 0 582 49276 9
Todd,M 1985 Roman Britain 55BC-AD400	Fontana	ISBN 0 00 686064 8